The Trials and Tribulations of a Fen

The Trials and Tribulations of a Female Taxi Driver

Beryl Armstrong

Beryl Armstrong

Copyright © 2023

All Rights Reserved

ISBN:

Disclaimer

Every word in this book reflects exactly what happened. One or two of the names have been changed to protect the identities of the individuals. Nothing has been added that should not be in this book.

Dedication

I dedicate this book to my mother, Margaret Evans, who – at the age of sixty-nine – passed away on the 8th of November 1993 from cancer. She was the best desk clerk in Gateshead. Also, to my sister, Janet Bradford, who passed on the 19th of March 2002, aged fifty-seven, from a rare brain tumour. Finally, it is also dedicated to Janet's grandson, Adam Bradford, who died on the 23rd of December 2019, aged just twenty-seven years, from the same brain tumour his grandmother had. If this book gets published, I would like to donate 20% of the sales to Marie Curie, Newcastle upon Tyne, and Brain Tumour Research, London.

A huge thanks to Trysten Joseph Gawthorpe for the illustrations in this book. He is eight years old.

Acknowledgment

To my wonderful partner, Kay, for the unwavering love and support during my battle with cancer and for believing in my book.

A heartfelt thank you to Jessica Grace Coleman for her exceptional editing skills in the initial stages.

To Trysten J Gawthorpe, a talented 9-year-old who spent hours drawing cars, leaving the rest to the professionals.

Gratitude to Karen Dean Wardly Taxis for the constant encouragement.

Special appreciation to Bookwritingfounders for their incredible work on "Trials and Tribulations of a Female Taxi Driver."

Thanks to Michelle Adam for her exceptional care, timely updates on my book, and her overall professionalism. She is truly a lovely and dedicated professional.

Table of Contents

Disclaimer 3

Dedication 4

Acknowledgment 5

About the Author 7

Introduction 8

Chapter One 10

Chapter Two 14

Chapter Three 21

Chapter Four 26

Chapter Five 32

Chapter Six 40

Chapter Seven 46

Chapter Eight 53

Chapter Nine 58

Chapter Ten 65

Chapter Eleven 66

The Trials and Tribulations of a Female Taxi Driver

About the Author

I was born in Scotland and lived there until I was fifteen years old. My father decided to move the whole family to Gateshead, Tyne and Wear, as he was moving to South Africa to build a business with his mate.

Once the business was up and running, he would then send for us all. Liar.

We found out after we had moved to Gateshead that he was off with the farmer's daughter. She was twenty-six; he was forty-one. He always said we would come to nothing in our lives.

Wrong. I became a director of a taxi company at the age of thirty-four years, having built a four-driver company to thirty-four cars. All my drivers were in uniform and very smart. I walked the streets of Gateshead, putting business cards through the doors every day until I had enough work for my drivers. Then, I did a full shift of driving till very late at night. Although my nickname from the drivers was "Little Hitler," I was well respected by the drivers. This is my story of nearly 38 years as a taxi driver.

I was married at nineteen, had one son, Anthony, and to this date, I have five grandchildren and four great-grandchildren. I am now retired and wonder how I had the time to work all the hours I used to work. I have met some really lovely people along the way, including a few celebrities such as Steve Cram, Steve Davies, Steve Ovett, Fatima Whitbread, and Paul Gascoigne (Gazza). I can honestly say I loved taxi driving; every day, I got a buzz at going on the road, as we called it. I had a very good sense of humor which has kept me going all these years.

Introduction

I was born in Arbroath, Scotland, on the 14th of February 1950, and I come from a family of five children – three girls and two boys.

Janet was the eldest, then came Michael, Stuart was next, and – last but not least – there were the twins, Mary and me.

As I weighed in at just 2 lbs 5 ounces when I was born, I was not expected to last the night. I was even given the last rites.

However, I survived, and now I'm here to tell the story of my life as a female taxi driver – a job I did for nearly thirty-six years. It was a tough line of work to be in as a woman, but it wasn't the first time men had ill-treated me.

My father used to beat me up at a very young age, and at just six years old, I was raped by a 15-year-old boy when we lived on a farm. This happened in the farmer's barn, and when my sister told my father about the incident, I got a good hiding – for being in the barn.

When I was fifteen, we moved from Scotland to Gateshead, Tyne and Wear. At this time, my father was on his way to South Africa to start his own business, but he never arrived. We later found out that he'd actually gone off with another woman – bastard! Though this was much to my joy, you'll find out why later in the book.

My first job was at Jackson Tailors, but when I reached the age of sixteen, I decided I wanted to be a nurse. So, I joined Bensham General Hospital as a cadet nurse; I did all the dirty jobs the cadets were given, but I loved every minute.

I then took the hospital test to start the training that would qualify me for the role of a SEN: a State Enrolled Nurse. I lasted until I was 18 years old – at which point I had six months left before qualifying – but then I had a massive row with the matron and resigned.

Looking back now, that was the stupidest thing I ever did in my life; I certainly regretted not finishing, but hey… we all make mistakes!

That is when I started my career in taxis, knowing only the one-way street in Gateshead.

Chapter One

My first job was as a booking clerk at Whitehall Taxis, Claremont Street, Gateshead. I loved working in the taxi office as I enjoyed meeting the customers who came in; I would always have a good chat and a laugh with them while they were waiting for a taxi.

Mary, my twin, had already passed her driving test and was the first female cabbie on the road. I was the second female cabbie, at the age of eighteen.

My first time behind the wheel of a car was when I was four years old in my father's Jeep; we were in a field, and he stood me on the seat so I could steer it. From that moment on, I knew I wanted to be behind the wheel of a car.

I begged Mary to take me out for driving lessons, but she never did. So, while I was working at the taxi office, I got another job in a nursing home on the night shift – 8 pm till 8 am. From there I would go straight to the taxi office and carry on till 1 pm. I continued to do those shifts for three years until I had enough money to pay for my own driving lessons, having twelve lessons that year. I took my test on the 11th of December 1968 and, to my delight, I passed the first time.

I already had a car lined up: it was an Austin A40 that I paid £15 for, but as it was for sale in Langold near Worksop, I had to travel on the train to collect it.

The drivers in the office took the piss good style, thinking I'd bought a banger, but they sure got a shock when they saw it, as it was immaculate. I still remember the registration: 0BB 909.

Due to the council rules, I had to have been driving for a year before I could drive a taxi and have a four-door car, but that didn't matter to me. At night, when I wasn't working in the nursing home, I would go to the office. If any customer was on their own, I would nick the fare and take them – only the desk clerk and I knew I was cabbing in my little Austin A40. I made what you'd call 'a few bob' in those days, so I saved up and then bought my first legal taxi: a Ford Cortina Mark 1, aubergine in colour.

Before going on the road, however, I had to insure it for Public Liability. I did not require a meter as it was private hire. The charge was twenty pennies (old pennies) per mile, and if we made five pounds all day and night, that meant we'd had a good shift.

If I had to describe myself at eighteen years old, I would say I was a bit of a tyrant and was a law unto myself. I was always breaking the speed limit, though luckily – on those occasions – I never got caught. I had no fear of anyone or anything.

On several occasions, I found myself driving men who did nothing but take the piss as I was a female driver. I would just slam the brakes on and tell them to fuck off out of my car. Boy, did they grovel for me to take them home! Most of the time, I would take them home; it was only the odd time that I would chuck 'em out and leave 'em.

While driving the taxi, I met my first husband, Henry Armstrong, who was tall, dark, and handsome. He was a bricklayer by trade, and I fell in love with him at first sight. He was like a younger version of Dave Allen, the comedian.

We were married on the 7th of February 1970, and a year later, we had a son, Anthony Stuart, who was born on the 3rd of March 1971.

I still worked as a taxi driver all through my pregnancy, but at eight months. I went back into the office on dispatch. It was while I was at work that I went into labour.

Tony was just two weeks old when I returned to taxi driving, and by this time, Henry had enlisted in the army, his first posting being in Germany. Unknown to me, Henry was a heavy gambler; instead of giving me his wages every week, he would go and blow the lot in the bookies and then tell me he hadn't been paid. So, my brother had a talk with him and told him: it's the army or your wife.

Tony was six months old when we moved to Germany, but we were only out there for six months. Henry was always on manoeuvres, so I was always on my own. There was the Captain's wife who lived in a bungalow nearby, but I hardly ever saw her. Then there was the Corporal's wife, who was just really stuck up; all she talked about was her husband.

I didn't like it in Germany. The flat we had was massive, so it was very cold in the winter. It had double glazing, but it wasn't like ours back in England; their double glazing featured a window, then a massive space, then another window, so it wasn't really warm at all.

We were due to come home for Christmas, and as my suitcases were on the top of a very large cupboard, I kept asking Henry to get them down for me, but with him, everything was always, "In a minute!" So, I reached up to get the case myself, and it went crashing straight through the window.

Jesus, the landlord was straight down to see what the racket was! I told him I'd dropped a box of glasses when, in fact, the entire window had gone. I had to pick all the glass out of what had once been a window and then put it in someone else's bin! I was laughing, because if anyone tried to clean the glass, their hand would just go straight through.

After going home for Christmas, I decided not to go back to Germany, as I just didn't like it there. So, I ended up staying at the family home with my mother, Janet and David, and their two children.

I bought another car and went 'back on the road', as we cabbies called it, seeing my husband about three times a year.

Eventually, things started to go wrong in our marriage.

One day, Henry went out for a drink with his mate, and his mate left his chequebook on the table – so Henry only went and filled in a blank cheque for himself! Well, the soldier reported Henry, and he did six months in Colchester prison for fraud.

So, when Tony was about six years old, we split up and eventually divorced.

Sadly, Henry died at the age of thirty-two. Looking back now, I say that we were meant to split up that way so I wouldn't have to go through the torment of looking after a sick husband so young.

While I didn't believe in handouts, and I was more than happy to support myself and my son, I was grateful for my wonderful family, who helped me look after him.

I was very happy just driving a taxi, though the one other thing I do regret in my life is that I missed a lot of my son growing up. The upbringing he had was quite strict, however, which I think did him well, and to this day, I am very proud of him. He has the utmost respect for me, and we've never had a cross word between us.

At this point, life was beginning to get pretty good. I made enough money on the taxis to keep my son and myself in clothes and food, so what else could I ask for in life?

Chapter Two

I worked at Whitehall Taxis until about 1975. In this was the same year Mary and Tommy were in the process of acquiring Gateshead Cabs. Mary, known to her friends as a "gadget queen," had an insatiable appetite for the latest technological wonders. Her latest fascination was a VHS VCR, a state-of-the-art tape recorder that could play films.

One day, as Mary and Tommy were busy with the affairs of the cab company, two individuals entered their office. These two characters were selling what appeared to be a brand new VHS VCR. Mary's curiosity got the best of her, and she couldn't resist the opportunity to own this cutting-edge device. The price tag was set at £100, and without much thought, Mary decided to make the purchase.

The VHS VCR came in a box adorned with a photo of the magnificent machine. However, amidst the excitement of the day's work, Mary didn't bother to inspect the contents of the box immediately.

It wasn't until hours later, at the end of their shift, that Mary finally decided to open the box and take a closer look at her new gadget. To her utter dismay and shock, the box contained not a VHS VCR but a pile of ordinary bricks!

The air in the office was suddenly filled with colorful language as Mary expressed her frustration and disappointment. It turned out that the two individuals who had sold her the "VHS VCR" were nothing more than clever swindlers.

The valuable lesson Mary learned that day was simple: Always inspect your purchases carefully, especially when dealing with dubious sellers. It was a costly mistake, but it left her with a story to remember and share as a cautionary tale.

Soon, Mary and Tom's company started to become quite the family business. My brother Michael started to drive with us, and Mum was on the desk. She was a very good desk clerk, and she remembered nearly all of the customers' names and addresses. They all loved her too as they always got their taxis on time. Stuart was the next of the family to join the company when he retired from the army as a sergeant major, and then Mary's son joined as a driver, and my own son joined as a desk clerk. So, we were one big happy family. We all seemed to get on very well, considering we were all living in each other's pockets, so to speak; we had the odd disagreement, but nothing to worry about. Mum was over the moon that we were all working together as a team.

To quote my father's words, "you bastards will never make anything of yourselves!" Well, how wrong he was. I hated him with a passion, not just because he was always beating my mother up, but because of what he did to me... as you'll find out in the coming chapters.

Life was great as a cabbie. I got a buzz going out on the road every day, sometimes even working from 6 am till midnight. Word soon spread that there were two female drivers working in the company, and – before we knew it – Mary and I were in demand, with women ringing the company to ask for a female driver. It annoyed the male drivers good style, but one or two of them were male chauvinistic pigs anyway. I soon told them where to get off, and they certainly didn't like that.

I was a good driver and had many compliments for my safe driving and – believe it or not – my courtesy.

We had lots of laughs regarding the customers – more so when you knew the husband was having an affair – but we never, ever informed their wives. The tips were always good when you picked them both up, and the husband would be panicking in case I let slip he'd been out with another woman the night before. Of course, me being the soul of discretion, I never said anything – I bet he was relieved when he got out of the car!

My Ford Cortina had now decided to die a death after being on the road for a few years, so I had to hire a company car.

I was given a sunny bright yellow Datsun/Nissan – you couldn't miss me if you tried, but I loved driving it. Mary and Tommy had their own mechanic to repair the cars, so breaking down wasn't a problem, but running out of fuel was – more so when I ran out of petrol with customers who were on their way to a funeral!

I had lent the car to a driver the night before, and he was supposed to replace the fuel he'd used, which the lazy bastard did not, so the result was I ran out. The air was blue with my customers' angry words, and needless to say, I never ran out again. When I next saw the driver, he got both barrels from me – mind, it didn't help that the fuel gauge wasn't working either.

New Year's Eve was fab to work; we always got tips galore as the customers were always in a good mood.

One New Year's Eve, I had to go to a pub called the Bensham Jockey, and this guy came up to my car and asked me to take his mate home. His mate was legless, so I said, "no chance – if he spews in my car I'm off the road for the night." Well, he soon got nasty, calling me a c**t.

I was livid. I got out of my new car and slammed the door. I then punched him all over the car park of the Bensham Jockey – and I must have hit him hard as my knuckles were bleeding. I said to the driver, who was with me, "thanks for your help," and he just said, "you were doing okay by yourself."

Another two weeks went by, and I had to go back to the same pub on a two-car booking. It was the same guy I chinned. He said, "I'm not getting in the same car with her; she's a psycho!" I just laughed and told the lads in my car what had happened. They told me, "you did right."

I had put my name down on the council list for a hackney carriage plate, and after seven years, I was top of the list, so plate number forty was given to me. Wow, did I think I was the bee's knees, now with a licence to hack fares from the streets! Mind, I always used to pick them up anyway – the plate just made it legal.

The Trials and Tribulations of a Female Taxi Driver

So, I started to go to the nightclubs in Gateshead, picking up fares from anyone who flagged me down. One Saturday night, these two lads flagged me down who wanted to go to Sunderland. Both of them had had quite a bit to drink, and they obviously thought they were clever. Well, if they thought a female taxi driver equalled getting a free ride home… how wrong could they have been?

One of the warning signs you learn in cabbing is that if customers leave the front seat empty, beware: they're probably going to do a runner at the end of the journey. Well, these two must have thought I was a right muppet! After listening to their crap, I decided they weren't going to pay, which was confirmed when one of them said, "what are you going to do if we don't pay at the other end?" Not a problem to me, son – I slammed on the brakes, pulled out my gun, and turned around to face them, holding it up.

The looks on their faces! "eh eh, we were only joking, Mrs," one of them said.

"Tough!" I said. "I'm not. I'll have £20 now, or you guys are walking home."

So yes, I got my £20, and I carried on to Sunderland. The fare was £15 in the end, so I gave them £2 change and told them I would keep the rest for my tip. After all, I'd had to put up with a lot of shit from them.

They got out of the car, calling me all the 'fucking bastards' you could think of, but I just laughed and drove off.

May I add, that was the only time I ever took extra money from a customer, but they deserved it. What you see is what you get with me, and that is how I think I survived in taxis for as many years as I did.

Now, here's the thing: some of the passengers would be right arseholes, who would get in the car and think they owned you, and more so when they were on a drug run. Oh yes, we had them too – you always knew when they were going for drugs as you never parked outside the house, always in the next street. Some of them treated the drivers roughly, but although we couldn't prove they were druggies, we knew the score. I didn't want to know what they were doing – just as long as I got paid. I always thought the police should use taxi drivers to get the dealers, as they know roughly where they all live.

The only time I got really annoyed with them was when they left dirty needles in my car. Once, a regular drug user of the firm left a used needle in the back of my car, and I went mental. The next time I picked him up, I told him, "If you ever leave a dirty needle in my car again, I'll keep it and stick it up your arse the next time I pick you up!" He couldn't be more apologetic, but I meant it.

I once took two of them to the central station in Newcastle. After I'd dropped them off, there was a phone call to the office; they'd only gone and left a parcel in my car. Was it drugs or was it money? That I will never know, but I did charge them for it as I was already back in Gateshead. They were lucky, as the next customer could have found the package and kept it.

1976 was a terrible winter, and we had so much work booked in, it took us twice as long to get moving. If I remember rightly, for about two or three days all the roads were closed, and it took me four hours to do ten miles – that's how bad it was. Besides, you probably know that driving on ice and in blizzards is very tiring.

I remember that I had to do a wedding once, but the snow was so bad I had to shovel myself about a thousand yards to get my car anywhere near the front door to pick up the bride. And, being determined that she wouldn't miss her big day, I managed it.

Some people are never fucking satisfied, though – they rang up the office a couple of days later and wanted a refund after I'd shovelled my way to the house. Apparently, I didn't get near enough to the front door. You can guess what the answer was – it ended in 'off'.

The Trials and Tribulations of a Female Taxi Driver

One evening, I had to go to Slaley Hall to pick up some customers. It was a terrible icy, snowy night, and the road to Slaley Hall was like a roller coaster. I got to the top of this hill, and it was a sheer drop to the bottom – it was that bad I ended up going sideways down the hill. My arse was going good style, as was my heart, but I managed to pick the customers up and drive them safely home. It took me three hours to do the journey, whereas in good weather it was a 40-minute run. On the way back, I was sliding all over the place, and more so when I got back to their street; trying to avoid all the parked cars was a nightmare. However, I got them home safely and managed not to hit any of the cars.

1977 was a strange year for me. It was the year of the Queen's Jubilee, and the Queen was going to be visiting Newcastle. As our taxi office was on the main road that she'd be passing, we decided to spruce the office up with flags and banners, so that when the Queen passed, she would see it. We also dressed ourselves up in the Union Jack.

Well, the drivers were going mental as neither Mary nor I would do any work until the Queen had passed our office.

One driver came out and said, "are you two fuckers going to get any work done?" and Mary and I said, at the same time, "fuck off! We're waiting for the Queen." It was lovely to see her pass in her royal car.

1977 was also the year Mum decided to emigrate to Australia, as Janet, David, and the two boys had emigrated there in 1970. Janet was always telling Mum she should go and live with them, so off she went to a new country and a new life. I was very upset, as we had never been apart, and this was the first time in my life that my mum was going to be so many thousands of miles away. However, we were in constant touch, so I soon got used to her living Down Under.

Even so, I missed her very much – so much, in fact, that three years later, she got a house for Tony and me, and we, too, emigrated to Australia. So, the three of us shared a lovely home, which was back-to-back with Janet's house.

I took some time out from cabbing and got a job as a store detective. Now, being a store detective was a completely different kettle of fish, though you still had to deal with the similar kinds of aggression you get with taxi driving.

On one occasion, I picked up a young lad for shoplifting, and when I got him back to the office and told him I'd be calling the police, he threw a chair at me. Luckily, a member of staff came into the office then, and the police were pretty quick to arrive.

While out in Australia, we were in constant touch with Mary, who wanted to see what was so special about Aussieland. So, she decided to come over for a holiday with her son, Allan, for six months. Janet and I kept it a secret that Mary was coming over – can you imagine Mum's face when Mary and Allan stepped off the plane? It was such a shock, especially as she'd been expecting a friend of mine.

The friend she'd been expecting was very religious, so – for months – my mother kept going on about how 'I don't think I'll be going to church all the time she's here.' Hell, I thought my mother was going to have a heart attack with the shock of it all!

We had a great time while Mary was there, but she kept nagging Mum to come home to England – the family was split up and we were all too far away to just hop on a plane every five minutes.

We did come home a year later. By this time, Tony and Janet's boys spoke fluent Aussie, but it didn't take them long to acquire the Geordie accent again.

Chapter Three

We moved back to Gateshead, where we all had flats in the same street. I went back to cabbing, and this time I hired a Hillman Hunter from Mary. It was automatic, but it gave me so many problems – in the winter, the bloody thing wouldn't even start! Mary, on the other hand, had just bought a Nissan Bluebird.

I was on earlies, and one day, the car wouldn't start. I had to phone Mary up at home to get a jump-start, and well… she was in the right mood, shouting, "what the hell have you done to it?"

So, I shouted back, "it's a heap, that's what! Just come down and give me a jump-start!"

Boy, was she mad! "How the hell can I give you a jump?" She yelled back. "It's a Japanese car and the battery is in fucking Japanese!"

"Well, you clown," I said, "the terminals are still the same!"

I never let her forget it. I even nicknamed her 'Yoko' and, even to this day, I still call her that. Her partner Tommy had the same car and I nicknamed him 'Chairman Mao.' So, those were the bosses of Gateshead Cab Company: Yoko and Chairman Mao, driving 'Jap crap' as I called it.

Every taxi driver has a nickname in the trade, and you will find out mine soon enough.

While I was in Australia, my hackney carriage plate had been put on my brother's car, as that way I wouldn't lose it. So – much to my delight – when I returned home, I was back on top of the list and I received a second one: HC 84. It was put on my own car as I'd been in the trade for seventeen years and I thought I deserved a second plate. I was over the moon at having two plates, especially with me being female!

By this time, Gateshead Council had started to take over the private hire cars, and they all had to be tested once a year to make sure they were roadworthy. Mary's other Datsun had started to look a bit tatty and needed some welding done on it, so her mechanic decided to do just that – but in the street.

Well, the next episode was Jeff, the mechanic starting to do the welding, while I was in the office, having a coffee. Soon, in came Jeff, looking ever so sheepish. He shouted for Mary, but Mary took no notice of him, so once again, he shouted her name. Well, she carried on talking on the phone and ignoring him when, all of a sudden, he bellowed, "Mary! Phone the fire brigade! The car's on fucking fire!"

I couldn't stop laughing; he'd only gone and set the seats on fire when he was welding, and – to crown it all – he'd left the acetylene bottles right next to the car. He could have blown the whole fucking street up!

"Jeff," I said, "shift the fucking bottles before we all go up in flames!"

He did manage to move them before the fire brigade arrived, and he was very lucky he didn't get fined for welding a car in an open street. Sadly, the little Jap Crap was towed off to the scrapyard, never to be seen again.

Mary was bawling her eyes out, so I said, "what's the matter? It was a piece of shit anyway!" That's what I thought of foreign cars.

Yes, taxi life was not just about making money. We had laughs, and we also cried when we lost good cabbies – we lost a few in those years, and one or two of them were very young. We also lost good customers.

I remember a very sad time, when I used to carry this lovely family back and forth to the hospital with their young baby. He was a lovely little chap who had heart problems, and the poor wee soul died a week before his first birthday.

We went to his funeral, and I cried so much for him and his parents. We ordered a lovely teddy bear for him; all the drivers put their money towards his teddy bear wreath. It was a nightmare, and we all felt for his parents, even though we couldn't even imagine what they were going through. We would say our company was a family one, as we cared for the customers and got to know them so well.

I once picked this drunk up from the office, and he said to me, "you know, one of these days, you are going to get raped." Well, that statement was like a red rag to a bull!

I was crossing the Tyne Bridge at the time, and I slammed on my brakes and he slammed his head off the windscreen – there were no seat belts in those days. I said, "are you the fucker who's going to do it then?" And he said, "no, no!"

I said, "get the fuck out of my car and walk!" as I kicked him out of the taxi.

Girls, however, are the worst passengers. Jesus, they always want to fill you in when they're mortal drunk. I would rather take four drunken men home than two drunken girls.

Generally, though, I loved my job with a passion. If I picked up a fare who didn't have enough money, I always made sure they got home safely, and more so when it was young girls.

I was working from Heworth metro station late one night when the inspector came up to me and asked if I would take a 15-year-old girl to East Boldon. This was 12 pm at night – what was a 15-year-old doing prancing around at that time of night?

She didn't have the fare, and she said she'd have to go to Washington as her father would kill her for being out at that time of night. So, I agreed to take her as she said her sister would pay me when we got there.

The sister, however, had no money. The fare was £4.90 then, so I gave her two weeks to come to the office with the fare.

Well, there was no sign of it, but six months later, I was on my way to East Boldon at eight in the morning, so I decided to call this house where the girl said she lived. I did get my money, but her father was furious, and I heard him shouting at her. She certainly learnt her lesson: don't bump Beryl for the fare. She always catches up with you sooner or later.

There were occasions when you would pick up a fare and you wouldn't get paid, but these were few and far between. Calling the police was always a waste of time and money; they were so busy that by the time they came, you could have made up the lost fare, so I never bothered. It was best to just cut your losses and carry on.

Sometimes I would work from the Tuxedo Royale, as it was known then: a floating nightclub on the Tyne. One night I picked this young lad up, and he seemed okay and quite talkative, so I thought I'd have no worries getting the payment from him. Wrong!

On the journey home, he was bragging that he'd paid £80 for the shirt he was wearing – so there was another reason not to mistrust him – and the fare was only £2.90, which was not a lot in those days, considering he would have spent a fair few quid on the boat.

Well, as we stopped, he started to fumble with the door handle, so I knew then that he was going to run. He started to make his exit, but I caught his £80 shirt by the neck and ripped it off his back as he was preparing to dart out of the car. He then jumped the wall and was off without paying.

I was fuming, but I had a good laugh about the shirt on the way back to the boat. He was the only person to ever get away without paying the taxi fare in my cab.

I did enjoy working from the boat, and at the time, I was the only female cabbie down there.

I remember working there late one night, when there was a party of lads from Carlisle out on a stag night. One of them had a bit too much to drink, so he decided to come off the boat and stand beside the hot dog stand. He then decided to have a pee, but he lost his balance and fell into the water.

It was a right rough night, pouring with rain, and the currents were strong. All the cabbies were trying to throw him a rope, but he kept missing it, and then he went under… before popping up again.

One of the lads was going to jump in after him, but I said, "Don't be stupid; the current will take you," so we all shouted at the kid, telling him to grab the chain above him. He couldn't reach it, though, and under he went again.

Sadly, this time, he didn't come back up.

After that incident, the hot dog stand was moved and the owners of the boat put a safety net all the way around, in case it ever happened again. It was a terrible night and it's terrible to see someone drown when there's nothing you can do to stop it.

When I went home, after giving my statement to the police, I felt sick as a dog. It was awful seeing that young man drown right in front of my eyes. I couldn't sleep, thinking of him, and I kept wondering if there was anything else we could have done.

It was two weeks later when they found his body.

Chapter Four

It's amazing what cabbies see when they're driving around. I remember my sister was out on a cab run one night, and it was very late when she passed by this house in Pelaw. She told me the house was on fire and she called the fire brigade, then she got out of her car to try and raise the family. She ended up kicking the door in and getting an old man out; he was very lucky that night that she was so observant, and that she had the nerve to kick his door in and get him to safety.

Another time, Mary was taking this young lass home and, at the end of the journey, the lass paid Mary but then said, "I'll give you a tip if you give me a kiss." Well, Mary came back to the office full of hell as she told me the tale.

I said, "what did you do then?" and Mary said, "I punched her in the face and kicked her out of the fucking car!" So there you go. I take it my twin is homophobic.

I did enjoy working late, and from the boat, but in later years, more women started to come into the 'trade,' as we call it.

I used to love working Christmas; it was the only time of the year you never got any abuse and the tips were great. Everyone was always so happy when you picked them up. Even if you were running late, they were brilliant and never complained, but they were always glad to get where they were going.

I put myself down to work every Christmas; after I'd spent time with my son, I would go out on the road for the day.

Back in the day, on New Year's Eve or during big occasions like these, we used to work twenty-four hours straight. But you know what? Nowadays, that's just not on anymore. Can't do it.

Anyway, back in the day, New Year's Eve was a right mix of excitement and being on your toes. It was awesome, no doubt, but we had to keep an eye out for some dodgy customers. It wasn't your regular day gig, mind you.

On New Year's, anyone and everyone could hop into our cab, not just our usual crowd. The offices in the city were shut, so folks would ring the first taxi they could find, and let me tell you, we had some real characters in the backseat. It was a wild ride, I'll give you that!

We all knew what that meant: either you had a good night, or you had shit all night, depending on how sloshed they were. They couldn't care less if they spewed all over your car, as long as they got home. My charge for spewing was £40 on a weekday and £60 on a weekend. After all, the car has to go off the road; nobody wants to get in a car that someone's just been sick in.

I loved working New Year's as everyone was always jolly and full of beans – though it was often a different story on the way back. Drunk, argumentative, and looking for a fight… we had it all that night.

I remember I once did a wedding, and this lady I was picking up had a lovely expensive suit on. They'd decided to give this elderly couple a lift home as it was on the way, and well… the old man had only gone and shit himself. It was all over my back seat and all over the lady's suit. I had to come off the road and remove my back seat to wash it. It stank so much, and it took two whole days before it dried out and I could use my taxi again.

I remember picking one chap up at 6 am on New Year's Day. He got in and I said, "happy New Year, good morning!"

He replied, "you're in a better mood than you were last night!"

"What are you talking about?" I asked. "I've never seen you before in my life!"

"Don't take the piss," he responded, "you took me home last night and were really aggressive."

So, I said, "I bet ya fifty quid I didn't take you home."

After arguing some more with the plonker, I eventually told him it was my twin who'd taken him home – though I never got the fifty quid, surprise,

surprise. His face was a picture, but that's what used to happen sometimes. Mary and I aren't identical, but we speak exactly the same, and customers used to get us mixed up; even Mum couldn't tell us apart on the phone.

Mary and I did everything together. We went on holiday together, and we both loved the bingo. We would go to work and, if it was quiet, we would nick off to the bingo. If we won, we would blow the shift, but if we didn't, we'd come back to work.

I remember going in at half-time one night and I shouted for £800, so Mary and I came back to the office and split it with Mum – not a bad night's work! We really enjoyed life, though we did have arguments now and again, and to this day, we are still very close.

I remember one Saturday night when I'd been on the road from 6 am, and it was now 3 am Sunday morning. I'd only had a couple of hours' break and the weather was really foggy. Mary got on the radio and asked, "Beryl, do you fancy a job in London?" To which I replied, "don't be a plank – I'm off to my bed!" We didn't worry about what weather we drove in, but at that time in the morning, I was just too tired to go that far.

So, the result was, we teamed up. I slept for a couple of hours while she drove for a couple, and then we'd switch, and that's how we went to London. However, as it was so foggy when it was my turn to drive, I ended up going the wrong fucking way – west, instead of south.

When Mary woke up, she went spare! Instead of the five hours, it was meant to take us to get to London, it took us seven hours. However, we made it in one piece and had a couple of hours' of sleep before heading home again.

We arrived back on Sunday night at 6 pm, completely wrecked. I went to bed and never saw the next day at all. That was my first long job in taxis, and I think the fare was £130 then, so it was a long haul for that amount.

My next long fare took me to East Kilbride, right up there in bonnie Scotland. We had a customer who'd lost her husband in a pit accident, and she'd received £20,000 in compensation, so had decided to have a good time with it. She weighed in at nearly 20 stone, but she was lovely.

She had started to use our taxis on a regular basis, and she got to know all the family, including Mum, on the desk. Well, she decided she wanted to go to East Kilbride for a week's holiday, and it was my turn to take her. In those days, we read a map if we wanted to get anywhere, and I asked Ian back at the office to direct me to the hotel in Glasgow. Well, he only had me driving up a one-way street! Luckily for me, I managed to do a U-turn before we could get hit by a double-decker bus that was coming straight towards me!

I drove her up to the Bruce Hotel in East Kilbride, a newly built hotel at the time, which was beautiful. She paid for me to drive her up, and then she booked me a room for the night, all expenses paid. The following week, I had to go and pick her back up, and again I stayed the night in the hotel. Really, she thought she was the bee's knees with all this money.

So, we pulled up at the hotel, I let her out of the car, and then I parked it in the hotel car park next to a Rolls-Royce, a Mercedes, and several sports cars. I walked back into the hotel and she said to the staff, "I would like a room for my driver." Blimey, I don't know what the staff thought, but I was only driving a crappy Hillman Hunter! I bet they thought I'd brought her up in a roller... if only they knew! The Clampets had arrived.

However, the next weekend I arrived to pick her up, and of course I stayed the night yet again, but the shock that was waiting for me was unreal. She had only copped off with the night porter – who was thirty years younger than her – and was bringing him back to Gateshead! I don't know how I kept a straight face, but there you are. I managed it.

They did, in actual fact, get married a couple of months later, when they had yet another taxi trip to rugby for their honeymoon. This time, Tommy had the pleasure, and he also had the pleasure, a few nights later, of having to tell the groom how to consummate his marriage. Absolutely true.

The honeymoon couple had only been home a month when they decided they would take a trip to Glasgow. This time, my mum was invited to stay at the George Hotel for a week. Well, who got the job of driving? Yes, you guessed right, I did.

The George was a very posh hotel indeed, so it was back to the same old pattern. I would drive up to the hotel and let them out of the car. Then I'd park it and go to the reception. We all then went to our rooms to freshen up. Well, I don't think they did, but I had a shower and a change of clothes and then met them and Mum in the lounge just before dinner.

Well, she spied on Max Bygraves, a comedian of the time, and she introduced me to him as her driver, before asking if we could have our photo taken with him.

Max politely said there was no problem, so she gave her husband the camera and we all sat beside Max. Her husband then proceeded to faff around so much that Max turned around and said to her, "Cor blimey, I could have painted a picture in the time he's taking!" Then he said, "never mind, love, I have sons of my own. I know what they're like."

In response, she said, "excuse me, Mr Bygraves, but that is not my son – he is my husband!"

Well, poor Max could have crawled under the table – he apologised and was off like a rocket! I was so pleased I was off the next morning.

The following week, I had to go back up to Glasgow and bring them home. After I'd dropped them off, Mum said, "thank the lord for that!" which we had a good laugh about. Mum said that all she ate in the hotel was whole lobsters – it must have set her back quite a bit every night.

She still used the taxis quite often, but then I think their money must have run out, as for a while, we didn't see or hear from them. I found out at a later date that she'd died of a heart attack, poor soul – must have been the lobsters she ate, because, by God, did she eat some.

That was the end of my long runs for a while – which was a shame, really. I felt like a queen getting waited on in those hotels, but all good things must come to an end.

Chapter Five

By now, the taxi company was starting to get quite busy, so Mary and Tommy employed a few more drivers. One chap called Danny started with us, and I didn't like him much; I thought he was quite an arrogant sod and he always had plenty to say about female drivers.

However, unknown to me at the time, he was to become my second husband.

We started going out together and, eventually, I moved in with him. God only knows why – maybe it was because he was good at fixing cars and DIY. Believe me, he wasn't much good at anything else.

His god was money, and he had a big opinion of himself, but – as you know – love is blind. So, it took me by great surprise when I married him a year later. This was, as it turned out, the biggest mistake of my life – as you'll soon discover.

My twin turned around on my wedding day and said, "You'll last three months if that." I should have listened to her.

Mind, on the day of the wedding, I fell down my mother's front steps – so that should have told me something. However, we not only lasted three months but three years.

We'd only been married a week when the police came looking for him. He drove a Granada, and he was having trouble with a brake calliper on his car. It was Christmas, and as everywhere was shut, he decided to help himself to one from a car of the same model – a car that was parked in the car park behind the Belle Vue pub in Low Fell.

Well, what he didn't bargain for was that he was being watched by a resident, who immediately called the police. Danny got away with a fine, as he told the police he was trying to get a tyre for his spare.

Can you imagine how dangerous it would have been for that driver if he'd managed to swap callipers? He could have killed the guy! But that was Danny – he just thought of himself and money. To this day, I think only he and I knew about it.

He was also a right-speed merchant, always getting caught for speeding. At one stage, I think he had twelve points on his licence.

Mary and Tommy had a grocer's shop in Dunston, and they opened another office above it. So, they decided to sell Gateshead Cab Company, which by now had been in the family for years.

Danny and I thought we would give it a try. So, at thirty-five years old, I found myself being a director of Gateshead Cab Company – stick that in your pipe and smoke it, Father Paedophile Evans. We only had four drivers, as the rest of them went to the new office Mary and Tommy had opened up, GODA Taxis (Gateshead Owner Drivers Association), aka Yoko and Chairman Mao.

This was in 1985, and by this time, a few taxi offices were starting to open. It was also the year the Yorkshire Ripper was loose, and – as he was supposed to come from the North East – most women were worried about going out and about late at night.

The tape recording that was sent to the police by that man saying he was the Yorkshire Ripper… that was scary, especially as his voice was pure Tyneside, meaning he could have come from any of the cities, towns, or villages in our area.

I remember, one night, I picked this guy up who was very creepy. He didn't speak, and when I asked him where he was going, he said Silverhills. Well, Silverhills was out in the middle of nowhere – just fields, trees, and the odd house. So, I was very wary of this creep, and more so when he started to ask me what a woman was doing a job like this for, and commenting on how I must pick up some characters.

Just as he said that, the radio blared out again about the Yorkshire Ripper, playing his voice.

My passenger said, "You must be vulnerable on your own in a taxi with men," and I replied, "I don't have any problem; I can handle myself, thanks. I'm a black belt in karate."

The night was bad; it was raining, we were surrounded by thick fog, and I had this creep in my car!

I asked him to direct me to where he lived, and by this time, I was shitting myself, my heart going ten to the dozen. My hands were sweaty and I was shaking inside.

He told me to turn right into a field and then along a dirt track – well, now I really was shitting myself. Then he told me to turn right into another field, where the trees were overhanging. We dropped down into another field and I thought: This is it, I'm going to get raped here – or worse. The only thing in this bit of field was an old-fashioned cart.

I squeaked, "Where is your house?" and he said, "Through those trees."

He put his hand in his pocket and I thought: Here it comes, a knife!

I'd put my car into first gear, ready to go, and then he pulled out… several pound notes. Well, was I not relieved! He paid me and I was out of there like a fucking bullet – never in my life had I felt so scared.

That is when I decided to protect myself, and I managed to get my hands on a Webley gun. It was never loaded and it didn't work anyway, but it sure frightened the life out of some of the idiots who tried to get away without paying. You never knew who you were picking up as a hackney carriage driver – at least when you were working from an office you got a name and address.

One day I received a phone call from Tyne Tees Television; they were looking for female taxi drivers to go on a chat show about women who did dangerous jobs. So, I went along with Pearl and Mary, two of the other drivers.

We arrived at the studio and met the person who would be hosting the programme – a young, upcoming Eamonn Holmes. He walked on the stage but had a slight problem, which I don't think he'd noticed – the zip on his trousers was broken. But Pearl sure noticed it and shouted down to him, "Eamonn, your fly's bust!"

Well, poor soul – he had to go offstage and change his pants before we went on air. Bet he doesn't remember that!

Not long after taking over Gateshead Cabs, it was about 1 am when this lady came into the office looking for a taxi. She was mortal and she asked if she could go to the toilet. Well, the toilet was in the flat just behind where the desk clerk was working, so I said yes and instructed her to go through to the flat, where she'd see the toilet at the back.

So, she staggered through the door, but she was that drunk she staggered right over to the cellar door, and a moment later, there was such a racket – she had only fallen down the fucking cellar steps!

Well, after about ten minutes, she got herself back up the wooden stairs, and I said to the desk clerk, "Get a fucking taxi quick, so she doesn't remember what happened and try to sue us!"

About three weeks went by and then in came the same woman – thank God she couldn't remember going down the cellar stairs! Phew.

Every morning, after the bus run, I would go to different streets and do a card drop. Danny never got off his arse to do anything like that; he was too busy with his bus. But the drivers still had to be kept at work.

By the time I'd finished, we had a lot of contracts with new customers, but then you have to keep them – if there's not enough work for drivers, they just leave and go elsewhere to work. I was lucky that my drivers stayed with me.

I even created a rota for long runs so that they all had a chance to do one. We worked out that a long run was £30 and over, so we started at driver number two and went down to number 34. Once that was complete and all the drivers had had a long run, it would go back to number two. As Danny had the eight-seater minibus, he wasn't on the list.

Whitehall Taxis were located a few streets away from us, and they were starting to get quite big – plus, they used to carry all the Jewish community around, and they used taxis every

day, so they were very busy. So, during the day, I walked the streets, delivering business cards door to door. Boy, was that hard on the feet – but it paid off as the business started to get busy.

So, we added to the drivers and ended up with 10 for the time being. I managed to get a lot of contracts, and even a good one for the 15-seater bus. We had to take fifteen Jewish children to Sunderland every morning and then bring them back at night, so Danny and I did one week on and one week off with that run.

I used to love doing it, even though the kids were little rascals, to begin with. I only knew my way into Sunderland and had to ask the kids to show me the way to the school; of course, they made sure they were going to be late for school by directing me the wrong way. As a result, on the first morning, I was twenty minutes late getting them to school – though it never happened again, I can assure you.

I got to know the kids and their parents very well, and we used to sing on the way to school every morning. The kids used to bring Jewish music with them and I would play it on the tape player. I liked it too, and they taught me the song. It went something like: shemabenee shemabenee musar ave aco vea vea titoise toirus immeca. To this day, I still don't know what I was singing, but I enjoyed it anyway.

Then I had a brainwave. I knew the Jewish people were careful with their money, so I decided to give them ten pence back for their phone call, and wow – business started to boom! We even pinched 90% of the Jewish community from Whitehall's office. They were starting to get worried.

On my regular trip to Sunderland, I started to carry one of the teachers; she was a lovely lass and we got on very well. In my experience, it is an honour to receive a tip from anyone in the Jewish community, but I always got tips from them, even if it was just 10p. It also takes Jewish people a long time to trust anyone, so I felt very honoured when I was invited to tea by the teacher's family – and even more honoured when she invited me to her wedding! What a thrill it was to be at such a lovely wedding.

Over the following years, I learned quite a lot about the Jewish community, especially about their religion.

One Friday, after dropping the kids off at home, I had to go and see one of the mothers. She had baked me bread as a thank you for looking after her children. I also found out why the men wouldn't get into my car if they were on their own; it was to protect themselves, as the driver could accuse them of something they didn't do. And the young girls always required a female driver. I could take the men if there was more than one of them, but otherwise, they would ask for a male driver.

Soon, we started to take their children to kindergarten every morning, picking them up again at lunchtime. We were so busy with them that, at one stage, we had six cars doing these runs every day – except on the Sabbath.

I, too, was very busy, finding myself on call many a weekend when one of their daughters was ready to deliver a baby. I remember being phoned at 2 am to take one to hospital, as she was in full labour. As they're not allowed to carry money on the Sabbath, I used to take them and then call back on Monday for the fare. They also weren't allowed to open a car door, carry a bag, or press a button on the lift, so I had to do it all – but I didn't mind as I respected their religion.

Before long, it got to the stage when, because we had so much work from them, we had to increase our drivers again. I then had to vet all the drivers who started for me, as I didn't want any prejudice against the Jewish people. So, whenever I started a driver, I would ask him what he thought, and if I didn't like his answer, then he didn't get the job with me. I had too much to lose if I started drivers who had problems with Jewish people.

They were a very generous breed, as we found out; every Christmas, all the drivers who did a kindergarten run got a lovely present from the mums, and then a very large box was sent to the office for everyone else. Most of it was kosher food, but there would be a couple of bottles of whiskey for the men and wine for the women. So, as you can see, they were very good to my drivers.

I always insisted that every driver should get out of his car and help his customers with prams, kids, and shopping, and I think that is why they liked using my company so much.

Taxis have changed a lot since those days. Now, my view of taxi drivers is that they are a set of fat lazy bastards who think the public owes them a living. I hate it when they pull up and just blast their horns. What they're doing is telling everyone that you're going out for the day or for the night and letting the thieves know that the house is empty. Also, what they forget is that some people are in bed having done a night shift, so they end up waking them up too.

I once picked up this man and asked where he was going. He was heading to the airport, but we never got to know the destination beforehand. "This is a two-bit firm, isn't it?" He said. "The driver doesn't even know where she's going!"

What an arrogant get he was! But then I explained that, as I had 34 cars on the road and there was a chance we'd have some crooks listening in to the radio, we didn't give the destination in order to protect the customer. All the crooks have to do is hear the address and that the guy is off to the airport – and, click! The house will be empty. So, for the customer's security, the destination was never given.

"I never thought of it that way," he said, to which I replied, "Well, we did," before adding – under my breath – "you plank."

Chapter Six

Most taxi drivers just worked in jeans and t-shirts, but we decided to have our drivers in uniform. So, as we had a tailor next door, I arranged with him to make navy blue pants for all the male drivers while the women were in royal blue. I then went to the shirt factory and bought two pilot shirts each for them, plus jumpers. The logo we had was a steering wheel, with the words 'Gateshead Cab Company' going around the wheel.

So, when all the uniforms were ready, we all wore the same thing, and they also had two of each to change into. My, were they smart, but the drivers at other offices just took the piss out of our drivers. I didn't care – I was proud of my lads. Every week I checked the cars to make sure they were nice and clean, which is why I got the nickname 'Little Hitler'.

Mind, we had a couple of plonkers working with us. One of them was Scottish, and he was either forever getting lost or taking the customers the long way around. So, if I had any complaints, I would do the journey myself, and if I discovered he'd overcharged, I would make him pay the difference back to the customer.

He was a rock 'n' roll fanatic and had a quiff in his hair. On one occasion, he overturned his car on the way to Newcastle, so when the lads were calling over the radio to say there had been an accident, he shouted down the mic, "It's me, it's me!" He had to crawl out of his windscreen and it cost him £700 to repair his car (which he didn't have, so he had to borrow the money from me). Afterwards, we nicknamed that stretch of road the Be-Bop-A-Lula Highway.

Another driver was once on a two-car booking and he was travelling along the road when he said to the customers, "I've lost the second car. Can you have a look to see if he's behind us?"

Jesus – both the customers were blind. So that went down well, I'm sure.

I once picked this chap up from the police station in Gateshead. He was going mental as he'd just been done for drink-driving. I said to him, "Well, had you not been so fucking tight you would still have your licence – and you still have to pay for a taxi home!" He wasn't impressed, but it was true.

I used to pick people up from houses who had been to parties. To keep the driver waiting, they used to say to me, "Do you want a drink?" and I would always say, "No thanks, I don't drink and drive."

"You're a miserable bastard," they would say, "one won't hurt you." But, as I told them, one drink for me is like them having four, so no thanks.

By this time, we were the first taxi company in Gateshead to introduce the company's name on the windscreen. It was done in the same colour as the uniform so that customers could easily pick us out.

We were also the first to introduce the eight-seater minibus service. That changed Danny a lot; he was a greedy twat to start with, but having a minibus made him even more money-minded. He used to buy a Chinese takeaway every night and never ever asked me if I had a mouth. His nickname, given by the drivers, was Slug.

All the drivers had nicknames. One was named Dick Turpin, as he used to come back to the office with anything he could get his hands on, had the fare not been paid. Another driver was called Dirt Bag. He used to disappear at 11 pm and come back at 1 am, having been off servicing the customer (if he fancied her). Another one was called Tiddles – he was the office cat. There weren't enough hours in the day for him.

I decided to buy an automatic car, and after about two months, the gearbox seemed to have a problem changing gears, so I took it back to the garage I'd bought it from. They had it in the garage for three days, and I finally got it back just in time for the weekend trade.

Friday was okay, but then – when I was doing my last run – I looked in the mirror to see smoke belching out the back. I dropped my passenger off and got back to the roundabout, but by this time, I couldn't see a thing out of the back window, so I stopped on the roundabout and got out to have a look. My car was on fire underneath and, as I'd had so much trouble with it, I just let it burn.

Then, a taxi driver stopped his car and came running over with a fire extinguisher, trying to put it out. I told him I'd called the fire brigade before adding, "What the fuck did you do that for? You should have let it burn!"

Well, along came the fire brigade to put out the fire. Then they got a loader to take my car back to the garage where I'd bought it. Had they done their job properly, instead of the botch job it clearly was, it wouldn't have caught fire; the oil from the gearbox had been dripping onto the exhaust, which started the fire. However, the garage had to repair it.

When I was younger, I never trusted garages to service my car, so here's a tip: before you book your car in for a service, put a small dab of nail varnish on any part you want them to replace. Then you'll know whether they've actually changed it or if they've just charged you for a part that's never been changed.

They're buggers, some garages. I caught one garage out of good style when I put my car in for a service, as the nail varnish was still on the parts – say no more.

After a while, every other company followed suit with the windscreen stickers and their logos. Although we were doing pretty well, however, most of the company's money went back into the business for advertising and replacing uniforms. We, as a couple, just about earned a wage, though it wasn't a bad one at that.

By this time, we had a lot of contract work, and we were taking on drivers to help with the extra work that was coming in. I remember one driver who came for a job. He could hardly speak English, and when I interviewed him, he said, "All I want is a job." He didn't even ask me how much he would make.

Another driver said to me, "You're not starting him, are you?"

I said, "Yes, any objections? Because if you're racist, you can piss off."

I also started another one who I think was from India. He was lovely – very athletic and had muscles like I don't know what. His name was Ashique, and he proved to be a real asset to the company, especially when a drunk was going to punch my lights out at the office. Ashy, as we called him, took the drunk out of the office and kicked him down the street, so he clearly didn't stand for any fools either.

The public doesn't realise how badly taxi drivers can be abused. One night, I had these three lads in the car who was really drunk, and one of them was trying to be smart; as I was driving the car, he pulled my seat belt around my neck. I had a habit of resting my microphone on my knee, especially when I had drunks in the car – well, I pressed the mic so the office could hear the crap I was getting and then threw my location for the desk clerk to hear. After about ten minutes, ten taxis surrounded me. That's one good thing about taxi drivers: they look after their own when there's trouble. We used to have a call sign and would give our location if we needed help.

Well, the lads got my passengers out of the car, got my fare from them, and then told them to fucking start walking – and it was miles from where they lived.

I went back to the office as I was really quite shaken up, and I never wore my seat belt again after that – only when I was private hire.

I had one driver whose passenger had a knife near his throat nearly all the journey; he was such a wreck after that he didn't come back on the road until he'd bought a black cab – that's how scared he was. Another driver had a gun put to his side but, luckily for him, the place he took them to was crawling with police, so they quickly jumped out of the car and scarpered.

Any idiot sitting in the back of a saloon taxi could stick a knife in the driver's back and, believe me, we picked up some right idiots through the years. Many a time, I would take fares to the police station; Newcastle was the best station as you drove through this arch and, as soon as the police saw it was a taxi driver, they came out to help.

One time I drove four of them to the police station and, when I got there, they said they were going to pay me just to make me look like an idiot. The copper said, "Right – one of you get out of the car, go to a cash point, and bring the money back," which they did. So I got paid, but the thing was, they were nowhere near where they lived – so I got my fare and then told them to get out of the car.

When they asked if I was taking them home, I said, "No chance – fuck off and walk!" and the copper just laughed.

One big contract we had was for the leisure centre in Gateshead, picking up celebrities for the Gateshead Stadium. So, when the games were on, we used to pick up the runners. Quite often, I would pick Brendan Foster up from his home in Low Fell. I also had Fatima Whitbread in my car, as well as Steve Cram, Steve Davis, and Steve Ovett, so we saw quite a few of the celebrities.

The first thing Steve Davis said to me was, "You can talk about anything except snooker."

It was great taking all these famous people around, especially as they were really chatty with the drivers.

One contract we used to do was the mayoral cars for the councillors – and what a pain in the arse some of the women were. Talk about snobs! We had to pick up four at a time and take them to the newly built Civic Centre.

Well, one old bat always used to complain that there wasn't enough room in the car, and I was driving a Granada by now – if she wasn't so bloody fat, she would have fitted in the car! I hated having to go and pick her up; can you imagine what was being said under my breath?

But another councillor, Kathy King from Birtley, was someone I really admired. What a woman she was – anything she could help you with, she would. Mary and I got to know her very well, and she helped us a lot later on when Mary opened Chowdene Taxis in Low Fell.

Kathy always said she'd like to go to Bosnia and take trucks of food, clothes, and medical supplies, and Mary and I were going to go with her, so we started to collect clothes etc. and store them up. We had the trucks arranged – with me and Mary driving one each – but unfortunately, the war broke out and we never got to go. Also, Kathy's husband was very ill and she had to look after him. This did, however, start us off on the track of doing charity shows, which I'll talk about later on.

Chapter Seven

By now, Danny and I were into our second year with the business and it was going very well. One day I had a visit from one of the girls from the Jewish college; three times a year, they all shipped out on leave, and they required taxis to take them to the airport, train station, and bus station. We discussed what the fares would be for each station, and she arranged to come and see me the next day with a list of everyone who was going away.

Well, when she brought the list round, I nearly passed out – there were three hundred of them and they all had to be moved within forty minutes! At the time, we only had ten drivers, but I had a brainwave. One of the drivers had a mobile home, and I asked him if we could borrow it to shift the suitcases. "No problem," he said. And, as one of the desk clerks could drive, I got him and another clerk to move the cases. Well, talk about a laugh – the mobile home was full to the brim, as Jewish people do not travel light!

So, that left the drivers to move the customers. It was just as well it was 6 am and there was no traffic!

Also, I had arranged for all the cases for the airport to be left at a certain number in the street, and for all the cases for the station to be left at a different number – and the same for the bus journeys. That way, no one would lose a case.

In the end, it worked very well, and we moved them all in forty minutes, so we got the job three times a year.

One thing I did notice, though, was that when we pulled up at the station or the bus terminal, there would be a Jewish gentleman watching at every point, so it's clear that they really look after their young girls.

The next time we made the same trip, I used a truck that belonged to another driver. It was so funny, as there were that many cases on it, the desk clerk had to lie flat on the top so they wouldn't lose any. Once our drivers increased, it was a lot easier to move them all. I think the drivers were relieved, too, as they didn't have to lift heavy cases into their car boots.

As I mentioned, as time went on, we increased our drivers to thirty-four, but I have always maintained that a taxi company can give better service with ten cars than it can with a large fleet.

I must also point something out. Most customers think that when a taxi is late, it's nearly always the desk clerk's fault. Sorry, folks, but nine times out of ten, if a taxi is late, it's because there could have been an accident on the road.

Another common reason is you – yes, you, the customer. Instead of booking a taxi from A to B, you will go out at night, come home, and then commandeer the driver to take your babysitter home, which is extra time on the journey. And, if that car is already booked for another run, the clerk then has to find another driver for the run she'd planned to give to the driver who is now taking your babysitter further than expected.

Also, a driver gets booked to go out, and then they end up going all over the world to pick up their mates. So, in the future, tell the clerk how many pickups there are, and you never know – next time, someone else's taxi will be on time.

I have also worked on the desk, and you wouldn't believe the abuse you receive over the phone! I'm sure the person giving it would not like to be on the receiving end. It is a very difficult job to keep all the drivers on the road and to make sure every call is on time.

One nightmare is the bingo queens – they're never on time, but all hell breaks loose if the car is late for them. And I'm sorry, folks, but we cannot drive the car into the bingo hall, so if you're playing the bandits and it's to hell with the taxi waiting outside, my advice is to get your backside to the door and not on the bandit.

Next, we have the customer who is moving. 'Can you send me a taxi, please? I'm just moving a few things,' they say. And then, when you get there, it's not a taxi they want; it's a Pickfords truck. But we still used to move them – it's all part of the service.

On the whole, most customers were really good. We had one elderly lady who was lovely. She loved to go and watch cricket, and she never, ever, missed a test match at Jesmond. Her only living relative was her niece, who lived in Walker. Every Sunday, we would take her to visit her niece, or the niece would book us to bring her to Gateshead to visit her aunt. They were a lovely pair, and they got to know all the drivers – to the point where she wouldn't use any other taxi company.

By this time, she was 89 years young, and soon it was to be her 90th birthday, so all the lads decided to have a collection and send her and her niece for a meal at the Springfield Hotel. I was to pick her up and drop her back off at no charge, and we also had a spray of flowers for her.

As I used to subcontract a lad who ran Rolls-Royces for weddings, I decided I would send her out in style. So, I rang my friend up and booked the Roller for her birthday – the only drawback was that if he pulled up, there was no way she would get in his car, as she didn't know him. So, I arranged to meet him at her house the night of her birthday.

I had the flowers in the back of my car, and I went to the house to pick her up. On the way out, she spotted the Roller and said, "My, Beryl, what a beautiful car that is behind yours!"

I said, "Yes, it's a Rolls-Royce. Have you ever been in one?"

She replied, "No, never."

Then I said, "Well, tonight, this is your car!"

You should have seen her face; it was worth all the money I'd paid for her to have it for one night. She started to cry as she sat in the back of it – she was so small her feet didn't touch the floor. As the tears were running down her face, I presented her with the flowers. It was lovely to see a little old woman so happy.

She even got the driver to come past the office so she could wave to them all on her way home, and for months all she talked about was this car and the lovely meal she and her niece had, compliments of 'the Gateshead cab drivers.' But those were the days when cabbies were proper cabbies; they're a different breed these days.

One of our drivers, Billy, was the right character. He could never get out of bed in the morning, and he always looked as if he'd just rolled right out of it, his hair sticking up in all directions. We used to take the piss right out of him, but no one ever got away without paying him the fare. The things he used to come back to the office with! There were watches, rings, cameras… he even came back with a television one day. And can you imagine the look on the drivers' faces when he rolled a motorbike into the office?! The customers always got them back when they came to pay the fare, which they always did.

We were always playing pranks on each other. One day, I went out of the office to go on a job and, when I tried to reverse the car, I discovered that the bastards had only put ramps behind the back wheels! The way my car was parked, I hadn't noticed them when I got in. They all came outside and were in stitches.

Another time, we were larking about, and they knew I hated heights, so they picked me up and plonked me on top of a high bus shelter! Well, being only 5 ft 1, I couldn't get down. The next thing I knew, a double-decker bus was pulling up, and – much to my embarrassment – there were only two of my customers sitting upstairs! The next time I saw them, I certainly had some explaining to do, but we definitely had a lot of fun.

The next trick would be to nick your car keys and move the car while you were having a coffee, so when you came out of the office, you thought someone had stolen it. But then, me being Little Hitler, I put paid to that – I had a security camera installed.

Taxi offices are usually scruffy holes, and ours was no different, so I said to Danny that the place needed a revamp. I picked the wallpaper and Danny picked up these lads who'd been revamping an office nearby. The lads told Danny they had enough material to make our office look class but that it would cost £1,000. We decided to go ahead with the new look, and it looked mint when it was all done.

I took a day off to paper the walls and the drivers helped me; as one came in from a run, I would have him helping me put up a strip of wallpaper, and then he'd go out and another would come in and help me out some more. We had such a laugh. Even though my nickname was Little Hitler, the drivers had a lot of respect for me as I would never ask them to do what I wouldn't do myself. If there was no night shift driver, for instance, I would do it. If the drivers needed help with money towards repairs, I'd help them too. We really did have an amazing bunch of drivers.

1983 was the year of the Ministry strike, and one day I received a phone call from the Ministry of Social Security, asking if I could supply taxis for their workers who were going to work – but I was informed that we'd have to cross a picket line. I said that I'd have to ask the drivers and get back to her.

Some of the drivers said yes, and others said no chance. It was a lot of work, too, as we had to pick them up at 6 am and then do another run at 2 pm before having another pickup at 1 am.

There were ten cars for each trip and we had to cross the picket line every time, which resulted in eggs and tomatoes being thrown at our cars, plus a load of abuse. At one point, I crossed the picket line, got out of my car, and said to the pickets (after they'd hammered me with rotten eggs), "I don't know what you're laughing at – these are getting fucking paid, you're not!"

After about two weeks, it was getting really bad. The strike lot had managed to find out where we all worked from, and they blocked the phone lines, so we couldn't get any calls coming into the office. It was a nightmare, as the other drivers – who weren't on the ministry runs – were complaining that they couldn't make any money. They even got a hold of my home phone number and started to threaten my 15-year-old son by saying they were going to come and burn my house down.

Tell you what – that was their biggest mistake, as when the bastards got back to work and things went back to normal, I gave them some stick right back. I got all their phone numbers and, one by one. I made sure they had no sleep for a week. I rang them every night at all hours of the morning – I even got one of my drivers to say he was having an affair with one of the striker's wives. He went mental on the phone and his wife sure got some stick.

They picked on the wrong people when they messed with my business, as after I'd waited a good six months, every single one of them got it in the neck. We used outside phones to ring them, and I kept ringing them for weeks on end at all times of the night.

One day, a female driver I had working for me was doing a run to the Metrocentre. On the way back, traffic was heavy and she was belting down the outside lane when she spied a fire engine coming towards her on the wrong side of the road. She managed to slow right down, but she still hit the fire engine head-on. She only suffered some whiplash, but she was done for driving without due care and attention and she ended up with a good few points on her licence. She packed it in after that, as it really shook her up.

I had another driver who was driving down Split Crow Road in Gateshead at about 11 pm when this drunken woman staggered out onto the road and he hit her with full force. Well, everyone in the pub came out and, eventually, the police and an ambulance turned up. The public slaughtered him by saying he was speeding at 100 mph – what a right load of crap. This driver was one person I knew who never broke the speed limit.

Unfortunately, the lady died two days later, but the police found out from other witnesses that the driver wasn't, in fact, speeding. This driver was so shocked that he went off work for six months. He did come back, but after he'd been on the road for a week, he realised he couldn't do it anymore. He was a man in his fifties, and thanks to this incident, his life was ruined; he had to give up driving.

Stannington was a very big institution for the mentally ill and, quite often, we would take customers up there if they had a weekend break. So, one day, I picked up this young chappie to go there. The place was just past Morpeth on the A1, and the roads that led to it were very creepy – and more so late at night. They were gloomy, narrow, lonely roads, and I didn't like going down them in the dark; they always gave me the willies. But, as it was my turn, I had to do the job.

However, on the way up, this lad told me he wanted to stop at a disused airfield, so I asked, "What do you want to stop there for?"

Well, here we go again…

I felt very uneasy, so I told the kid that I was sorry, but I had another customer to pick up when I got there. He kept insisting, and it took me ages to convince him – however, I managed to finish.

Chapter Eight

We were two and a half years into taking over the company at this point, and I'd say we were doing quite well. All the drivers were now in uniform, and we added another three female drivers to the fleet.

We had a married couple and another woman who was a lesbian; she was an excellent driver and all the customers liked her. She was always making comments to me, and I knew she fancied me rotten, but at the time, I just laughed and brushed off her comments – after all, I was Little Hitler.

At the time, I was thirty-four and had the figure of a 17-year-old with nice cleavage, so I suppose it was a compliment for my age.

Things started to go very wrong in my marriage around this time, so it's no wonder that I really turned into a woman. Danny just wanted me there to run the business, take all the flack, and keep him in brand-new cars, and I was getting really sick of being treated like a skivvy.

One night, we had a blazing row at home. Our gas fire was one that hung on the wall, and Danny bashed on it with such force that it fell off the wall and set the carpet on fire. He really was a headcase with a violent temper. If it was anything to do with the company, he just totally undermined me.

All of this led to me moving out of the house at 2.30 am and going into furnished accommodation. I walked out of my marriage with just a suitcase and nothing else.

I still continued to work at the company, but then he got himself a girlfriend and was just in my face all the time. I had to go and see him one day regarding the business, but he wouldn't discuss anything – all he said was, "Enjoy your girlfriend," so I replied, "Well, if that's true, it makes you look a right wanker."

So, I ended up going to work for Whitehall Taxis.

As Mum lived on her own, my son and my nephew moved in to look after her. I then moved into my girlfriend's place; I lived with her for three years and I was happier then than I had ever been in my life. Don't knock it till you've tried it; a woman knows what another woman wants. Remember, I'd been married twice before that.

Thank God my son is fine with it all, and my brothers. I'm not ashamed of it, either. At one time, I used to deny the fact that I was a lesbian, but now I simply don't care what people think.

I enjoyed working for my new company – and my partner worked there, too – so things were looking a bit brighter for a change. Then I decided to buy a flat and renovate it. This was my pride and joy, and I intended to give it to my son when he turned 21, but it was not to be. My ex-husband put paid to that.

He was useless at running the company and he was far too involved with his latest girlfriend; he just let the company go to the dogs. So, after a year of his incompetence, the company was a sheer mess, and he told me he was going to go bankrupt. He also said that they'd take my assets as I now owned my own property and I was still a company director. With this in mind, I decided to put the flat up for sale and put the cash in my son's name.

Unfortunately, it didn't work out that way. I used the same solicitor as the company and, when I sold the flat, they kept all my money for the company's debts. So, yet again, I was left with nothing. I should have put a notice in the paper to say I was not responsible for his debts, but I didn't know about that back then.

And, just to put the icing on the cake, the bastard sent his girlfriend and her pal to the house where I lived and, at 1 am, they made such a racket at the door that I went to open it – and when I did, they grabbed me by the hair and kicked the shit out of me. They got off with it, too, as when the police came, it just looked like we were scrapping.

But you know what they say: what goes around comes around. Well, I certainly had my day when it came to that bastard.

He was now driving for a company called Blaydon Taxis, and he had joined a lottery syndicate with some of the drivers. After being in this lottery syndicate for about two years, though, Danny decided to pull out of it at the end of July. Then, in September, the syndicate won £680,000, and he would have received a 7th share if he'd still been a part of it. So, I sent my ex-husband a 'With Deepest Sympathies' card, and inside it, I wrote: Sorry for your lottery loss of a share of £680,000. The money you did me out of was £63,000. What goes around comes around, you bastard. Enjoy your lottery win of £000,000.' I sent this card to the office where he was working, and as he opened it in front of the drivers, they ripped the piss out of him.

After that, Danny used to try and run me off the road with his minibus. And, years later, my son confessed something to me. After Danny had me beaten up, my son put out his bus windows – and his house windows.

After the beating I had, I ended up going to the hospital, and – a few years later – I had to have a hysterectomy, which I'm sure was down to the hiding I'd been given. Then, after they did that, my car was covered in nitric acid. There was no paint left on the roof, the bonnet, or the boot, and it cost me £500 for a respray – I swear it was down to him. After all, his pride was hurt; his wife had gone off with a woman.

After all that, I was left alone – thank goodness – to get on with my life. I enjoyed working at Whitehall, and the lads didn't have any problems with my sexuality, or that I worked with my partner. As a matter of fact, we used to have parties and barbecues at our house in the summer, which they all came to. It was great. One of the lads even had his engagement party in our garden; we covered the place with banners for them. God knows what the neighbours thought, but we always stopped the music at a decent hour, so no one ever complained about the noise.

Whitehall was a good company to work for, as we had a lot of long-distance runs. I remember doing a run to Grangemouth in Scotland one day. I left at

6 pm and arrived there just before 9 pm. I then dropped the goods off but decided to come back via Jedburgh Road, as it was half an hour faster than the A1.

On the way back, it was raining and quite dark, and I came across a young lass who was stranded with her car; she had got a flat tyre and didn't know how to change a wheel as she'd only just passed her driving test. She seemed quite naïve, and as nobody else would stop, I helped her change the wheel. The poor soul was very distraught, as all these so-called men had just driven past, even though she was stranded in the middle of nowhere. Anyway, after helping her, I gave her a business card and carried on back to Gateshead.

Two weeks later, I received a lovely letter from her parents, thanking me for stopping to help their daughter, which I was quite chuffed at. So, you men out there – next time a damsel is in distress, have a little bit of thought and stop to help her.

I'd been working at Whitehall for about three years when one of the drivers, who also had two brothers working there, had a massive heart attack. He was only thirty-five when he died, and he was such a lovely lad, too – it was a very sad time.

We decided at the office that we would put on a charity show for his family, and we held it at the Federation Breweries in Dunston. Well, what a show and what a turnout! We made £2,500 as the prizes were exceptionally good. We had two tickets to New York from British Airways, and BSM (the British School of Motoring) gave us two tickets for advanced driving lessons. Well, I won one lot that night, and my pal Mary – also a cabbie – won the second lot, which was very good for one night, and I'm glad that the money helped his family out a little.

After that, I put on another charity show at the Pelaw Social Club, this time for the heart foundation, but for this one I decided it would be fancy dress. So, of course, I turned up in Hitler's outfit. Frances Ritchie – alias Pearl – was one of the singers. She was brilliant, and she also comperèd the show for me. We also had a group who did the show for free; all I had to do was pay the roadies £100 to carry and set up the gear. My brother Michael also sang. He's an Elvis fan and loves singing his songs.

Pearl was very good at getting money out of the crowd, as it was all for charity, and she

never ever charged for her services – so thank you, Pearl, you were a star! After that, she did every charity show I put on, and we did quite a few over the years: for leukaemia, cystic fibrosis, cancer, and for the breast screening unit at the Queen Elizabeth Hospital. We raised about £20,000 for the mammography machine, which is now at Sunderland General Hospital.

I really loved doing those charity shows, but I never, ever, liked being in public view.

Thank you also to everyone who donated prizes; without them, we would never have made the money we did. Also, to all the clubs who gave us the function room free every time we put on a show, which we did every three months. We also did street collections, raffles, and anything else that would give us money for charity.

Chapter Nine

I had worked at Whitehall Taxis for about five years when the owners decided to sell the company. By this time, Gateshead Cabs had closed down, but Mary still had the lease on the building, so she walked back in and opened it right back up again, this time as GODA (the Gateshead Owner Drivers Association). So, once again, I found myself back working there.

We were there for another couple of years and then she decided to sell shares to the drivers, but that didn't really work as they all wanted to be the boss – stuff that for a lark! So, Mary then opened up another new company called Chowdene Taxis, based behind the Thomas Wilson Club. We had a porta cabin this time, and from then on, we held all our charity shows at the club.

I had some more hair-raising experiences when working at this company.

One night, I picked up this young lad to go to Washington. He seemed alright at first, but then he wanted me to drop him off on the side of the road, where there were no houses around, just trees. Well, he paid the fare okay, but then he dropped his trousers and got his willy out. I was so taken aback by his suggestion that I just said to him, "Put it away, son, and come back when you're older," before kicking him out of the car.

Another taxi was passing, and I knew the driver from Gateshead, so I explained what had happened. He just said, "Did you get your fare?" and when I said yes, he added, "Well, what are you worried about then?"

I was so mad, I called Felling Police Station and explained to a police officer what had happened. Well, all these coppers were just coming in, laughing, and asking, "Are you the one with the flasher?" I didn't think it was funny.

As a matter of fact, a couple of weeks later, a four-year-old child was sexually assaulted near the spot where I'd dropped him off, so who's to say it wasn't the same prick? That certainly put me off the police.

Talking about police, I was tanking down this road in a built-up area one day when I spotted a copper with a speed gun. He was just about to put it up to catch me when I slammed my brakes on – by the time he got the gun on me. I was doing thirty miles per hour, ha ha!

He just shook his head as I passed, and I drove by, just laughing my head off. Next time, bonnie lad, I thought. You just weren't fast enough!

Out of thirty-six years of driving, I got caught speeding just three times, and each time, it was for doing about forty-five miles in a thirty limit.

One night, I was driving through Low Fell towards the motorway with four lads in the car. I was in the outside lane when I looked in my mirror and saw a flashing blue light – it was the police. So, I put my foot down to get out of his way, and he pulled me over. I said, "Why have you pulled me over? I put my foot down to get out of your way," and he said, "It's you we were chasing." What a liar, and what a bastard – he did me for speeding.

One Sunday night, around midnight, I was driving down the A1 towards my office. I looked in my mirror and saw this car coming behind me like a bat out of hell. Well, just as he was overtaking me, I heard a bang. Thinking there was something wrong with my car, I braked very hard, and then the kid came alongside me. He hit the barrier, cut across the front of my bonnet, somersaulted, and ended up over the embankment, landing upside down. At the time, I wasn't wearing a seat belt, as hackney carriage drivers were exempt from wearing them.

I phoned the police, ambulance, and fire brigade as steam started coming from the car; I was sure it was going to burst into flames. So, I pulled over and got out of my car, and that's when I saw these two lads coming up the bank.

I asked if anyone was left in the car, and they said no, but then I saw a woman trying to crawl out of the windscreen. I went down to see if I could help, but as I'd just got back on the road from having an appendectomy, I couldn't pull her out, so I told her to crawl. I eventually got her to the top, and she was so covered in blood, I wondered how they'd gotten out of that crash alive.

I told them I'd sent for help, but one of the lads said, "We don't need an ambulance," even though one of the boys kept falling down. Obviously, he had hurt his leg.

And, with that, the three of them decided to do a shoot, making their way back down the bank towards Retail World. It never dawned on me that the car was stolen. By this time, the emergency services had arrived and they asked me where they were, so the police went to look for them and brought them all back to the ambulance.

There were now seven police cars, two ambulances, two fire engines, and – to top it all off – a police helicopter hovering above. What a waste of emergency services for these three toerags!

I didn't find out until the next day that the car had been stolen, at which point a reporter rang me at home.

Had I not braked hard when I did, they would have taken me down the embankment with them, and as I wasn't wearing a seat belt, well... I shudder to think what would have happened.

As ironic as it may seem, six months later – this time on the A184 – the same thing happened again.

It was 7 pm on a Saturday night and I had just picked up this lady and her four-year-old granddaughter. I had just joined the motorway again when I saw this car, completely out of control, behind me.

As he came past me, he started to smash into the barrier in the middle of the road, and the lady behind me started screaming; she thought we were going to get hit by the car that had hit the barrier.

Yet again, I braked, and yet again, he cut across my bonnet, somersaulted, and this time ended up actually on the fence, upside down – but this time, his passenger came flying through the windscreen.

I stopped my car, radioed for the emergency services, and then checked that my own passengers were okay before running over to see if the lad was okay. He was semi-conscious, so I came back to my car and grabbed the blanket I always carried in the back seat. I wrapped him up in it, but by this time, the driver had crawled out and he now had the guy's head on his lap.

"What are you doing, you idiot?" I asked him. "He could have internal injuries!"

By this time, the police and an ambulance had arrived. I was stuck right in the middle of it all, and to crown it all, when I got out of the car, I realised he'd caused a seven-car bump behind us – so you can imagine how much chaos there was. The copper asked how come he didn't hit me, and I said, "He nearly did!" My driving experience certainly helped me avoid a very nasty accident.

It wasn't until about an hour later that we were able to continue, and my passenger thanked me for a safe journey home, which was nice.

1993 was a terrible year for our family. Mum wasn't very well, so I made her go to the doctor for a check-up. She still worked on the desk for us, but she'd started to get very breathless, so the doctor sent her to the hospital for some X-rays.

Then the phone call came: the doctor wanted to see Mum as soon as possible. Well, I knew then – having been a nurse – that something wasn't right.

So, I took her back to the doctors, where she arranged for Mum to have some chest X-rays at the hospital. The next appointment she had was to go and see the consultant, so I took her to see him. When we got there, they wanted more X-rays of my mum's chest.

This isn't right, I thought to myself. They said they had lost the originals, but I knew.

When we went back in to see the consultant, he just looked at Mum and said, "I am so sorry."

I half laughed and said, "Mum thinks she's got lung cancer," and he said, "I am sorry to tell you that she has."

Mum asked how long she had, and he knelt down, held her hand, and said, "I cannot tell you that, but there is nothing I can do."

Mum just thanked him and we left the hospital. How I drove home with all those tears streaming down my face, I'll never know, and I didn't know what to say to my mother either; I was dumbstruck.

I got her home and called all the family to her flat. I then took some time out from taxi driving to look after her— as I was the only one who was single, I moved into my mother's home.

That night, she sorted her funeral out and everything and then she went into shock. I called the doctor out and he said she wouldn't last the night. He was wrong about that, bless her.

For a month, I lay on the floor next to my mother. I played her favourite music and talked to her, and eventually, she came round.

As I was due to go into hospital for a hysterectomy, I rang my consultant and explained the situation, asking if he would do my operation early. He was an angel; he had me in on the 4th of October. I had my operation on Monday and I was allowed out on Friday.

Being an ex-nurse, the doctor left me to see to my mother's morphine tablets, etc., and then, one day, she told me she'd put Mum on the morphine prematurely, so she asked me to reduce the tablets. After just a couple of days, however, I had to increase them again.

So now there were two invalids in the house.

She was a very brave lady, my mum. She never spoke about her illness and only once did she cry. She said, "What about my bairns?" Yes, even though her youngest was forty-three years old, she still called us her bairns. And then she said, "What about my programmes on the telly?"

Sadly, she died that November.

As I write this, the tears are flowing. She really was a wonderful mother and a lovely lady.

Not long after Mum died, Mary and I put on yet another charity show. This one was to raise money for syringe drivers, as the nurse said that when she got the one for my mother, she had an awful job getting hold of it. Fortunately, we managed to raise enough money to buy three of them; we were going to give two of them to the district nurses, and the other one was to go to the Marie Curie Hospice in Elswick.

Well, you can imagine my horror when I received a phone call from this woman at the Queen Elizabeth Hospital, asking me why I thought they didn't have enough. I said, "The district nurse had to phone all over to get the one they used on my mum," and she replied, "Well, I just want to let you know that I have a cupboard full of them."

Can you imagine my anger when she said that?

I said to her, "Well, it's a pity that the one they used on my mother didn't work!" I was so angry with this woman – her attitude just stank – so we ended up giving the lot to Marie Curie.

It was about three years later when I had to go to the Queen Elizabeth Hospital for something and guess what? This lady showed me to an office and, when I looked at her name tag and realised she was the same one who'd phoned me… well…

I was just about to stick one on her when the guy I'd gone there to see walked into the office – boy, was she lucky!

I said to her, "You don't remember me, do you? I'm the one who was trying to give you those syringe drivers."

Beryl Armstrong

Her face was a picture!

Chapter Ten

I remained off work until February 1994, and just two weeks after I went back to work, my taxi was stolen. I had popped into the house for a coffee, and when I came out, the car was gone – including everything in it. To this day, it has never been found. And, to add insult to injury, the insurance company refused to pay up, as I had three points on my licence and I'd failed to declare them. So, that was a £6,000 car loss.

The truth was, when Mum was ill, I had to renew my insurance, but when I got to the office, they kept me waiting for fifteen minutes, so I rushed through the form as I had a taxi waiting to take me back to my mother's. At this stage, she needed oxygen, and she didn't have the strength to give it to herself, hence my reason for wanting to get home fast.

I wrote to the ombudsman, trying to explain, but no joy. The best of it was the insurance company took a copy of my licence – so why didn't they ring me and tell me I'd forgotten the points? They sure as hell took my money from me every quarter.

It took me three more months to get back on the road, and that was with the help of my brother.

Well, that was short-lived too, as in October of that same year, I was rushed to the hospital to have an appendectomy – what a great year for me.

I eventually got back on the road the following year, and this time, I went to work at Dunston Taxis. My pal Mary worked there; we'd been friends for years and we got on very well. She was a lovely person. She was also built like a brick shithouse and she didn't care who knew she was gay.

We had some fab times at Dunston, and if I ever got into any trouble with the customers, Mary was always there to bail me out. We were the only female drivers at that office, and we got into some scrapes… what with the gambling and the one-armed bandits.

Beryl Armstrong

We had been introduced to the casino by one of the drivers, so on Friday nights, Mary and I would go to work, finish at midnight, and then off we'd go to the casino. What a nightmare! Sometimes we won but, most times, the casino won. I've seen myself blow my car payment and then work my guts out to get it back – or go back to the casino to win it back. And the bandits… You couldn't keep us off them!

That went on for a couple of years, but then I got wise and didn't go as much.

I did drop the bandit in the casino once – it was for £1,000. Actually, I dropped them five times. The first time it cost me £2, the second time it cost me £4.50, the third time £10, the fourth time £47, but what cured me was the fifth time – £800. I was on that bandit for 12 hours until I dropped it.

Mary's partner was with us then and she was drawing money from her bank account while Mary was winning on the tables. Then Mary's partner turned around and said, "Mind, if you don't drop it, you both owe me £400 each," so it was obvious she wasn't going to pay a third share of the money from the bank.

Anyway, as I said, I did drop it and, with the money Mary won on the roulette, we paid the £600 back to her partner and we all came away with £160 each. But my arse was going, thinking I owed her £400 – believe me, it cured me. I've never ever put that much money in a bandit again, and I don't even go to the casino now. It just shows you, you can get really addicted to those places, and you can get into a lot of trouble, too, if you own credit cards.

So, it was back to the bingo for us, but just one night a week – that was our pleasure.

It was great having a pal working for the same company. If you broke down, Mary was always there, and vice versa. She could do anything with a car, and for a woman, she could put the men to shame – especially when it came to DIY. She left the taxi trade to be a (very good) tiler, and she had her own business. We were friends for nearly twenty years, and not once did we ever have a wrong word between us.

Sadly, Mary died when she was forty-six, which was a terrible shock to us all in the taxi trade; there must have been fifty cars at her funeral. When it's the funeral of a taxi driver, they stop the traffic both ways, so all the drivers can pay their respects and follow the hearse.

It was now eighteen months since my mum had died, and her passing started to have some terrible effects on me. For one thing, I began to lose my short-term memory. I would be talking to a customer and, all of a sudden, I couldn't remember what I was going to say. Then, even though I knew where they lived, I would take the wrong road and the customer would say, "Where are you going, Beryl? You've passed the turn-off!"

Also, when I was at home, I would do things like putting the milk in the oven and the washing in the bin. I would be looking for something in the house and, although it was right there in front of me, I wouldn't see it.

I started to get very worried about this, so I took a trip to see my doctor, who was brilliant. She told me I was suffering from deep depression after my mother's death.

It was six weeks later, after seeing the doctor regularly, that I eventually told her about the abuse I'd experienced at the hands of my father when I was twelve years old. For thirty-five years, I had kept a secret from my mother that my father had raped me and that, for three years, he had continually sexually abused me.

When you read this, I'm sure you're going to say, 'How do you keep that a secret? Surely, your mother must have known!' Well, she never ever knew.

We used to live in Scotland, where he was a rep. Every other Saturday, he took Mum shopping and he would make sure I was left at home to do the housework. He would tell Mum he was going to see a client and then he'd double back home – and that's when it happened.

I dreaded this happening every fortnight, but I was too frightened to say anything. After all, in those days, who would have believed it? He was Jekyll and Hyde – the biggest bastard ever to walk on two feet – and I hated him with a passion. If I'd been old enough, I would have run away.

You just had to look at him and he would belt you for nothing. He was Mr. Nice Guy, though, to his family – and, incidentally, most of them live here in Gateshead. That's why we came down here, so Mum would have some family while he was supposed to be in South Africa. But, as we know now, he was actually off with a 26-year-old widow, one of his client's daughters. The best of it is my twin was going out with her brother, and my father forbade her from seeing him again – and now he's a millionaire.

That was the second time in my life I had been raped. The first was that time when I was six years old and had been playing in the barn with my brothers. There were some 15-year-olds there, too; one of them grabbed me and the other held me down, and he raped me. I think my brother came into the barn and got them off me, and – as I said before – when my father found out, I got a good hiding.

Also, when I was six years old, my father made me get into a stone-cold bath in the middle of winter. There was no central heating back then, as we lived in a hotel. Mum worked in the hotel for no wages – just the rent for the flat we were living in. She didn't know about the bath thing either. He warned me: "Tell your mother and you will get a good thumping!"

I can't really remember my childhood, apart from the abuse, and once I'd explained this to my doctor, she recommended counselling – and I agreed. So, for two and a half years, I went for counselling, sometimes three times a week, and my counsellor got me through some very bad times.

And, may I add, I did it all cold turkey – with no drugs or antidepressants. No thanks, not for me.

One thing she did say was that I had a very good sense of humour, and I think that had been my lifeline. I will say this: it was probably the hardest thing I've ever done, next to cremating my lovely Mum, but I'm fine now and I've lost all the anger I had inside me.

After that experience, I found I could talk openly about the subject. Not that I used to tell everyone, but now and again, I came across a customer who had a relative who'd been abused, and I would give them some advice.

I remember picking up this young lad once. He was about eighteen years old and, for some reason, he started to tell me about his experience. So, I advised him to go and see a counsellor – after all, they are well-trained.

Mine ended up leaving the job, but to this day, we remain good friends, and she still rings me up after all these years.

It was while I was working at Dunston Taxis that I had the pleasure of meeting Paul Gascoigne – or, as you all know him, Gazza. Well, don't listen to all the things you hear about him; he is a lovely lad. He was very generous, and he respected the taxi drivers. Every time I put on a charity show, he always came up with either a signed shirt or a couple of signed footballs, depending on the club he played for. I really don't have a bad word to say about the guy.

I knew all his family, and you couldn't meet a nicer family either. I had to pick his mum

up once from the house he rented in Seaham – blimey, that was some pad! As I drove in it had electric gates, so I pulled in, got out of my car to ring the bell, and who opened the door but Paul? He invited me in while his mum was getting ready.

I had to laugh as he had his dressing gown on and was busy wiping down the benchtops in the kitchen; I think they'd just finished a meal. For a bloke, he was spotless. He also offered me a drink, but I declined as I was driving. I started to laugh then and said, "It's something to keep me awake I need!"

Well, he went to the fridge, handed me a can of Red Bull, and said, "That will keep you awake."

And it bloody did, too – it kept me awake all night! When I got to bed, I couldn't sleep at all, so the next time I saw him, I said, "You, ya bugger, that Red Bull had me awake all night!"

Mind, while I was there, he never touched a drink himself, even though everyone else was drinking.

I also got to know Jimmy Five Bellies – another really nice guy. If Paul ever couldn't give me things for the charity shows, then he'd send them via Jimmy. As I said, he never forgot.

One Christmas, I picked Paul up along with one of his friends, and he asked if I'd been busy. I said, "Not really, very poor for a Christmas," so Paul said, "Tell you what, Beryl – whatever's on your meter, I'll match it." Well, it said £57, and when he got out of the car he threw £60 on the seat, so he's clearly a very caring and generous lad.

The thing with Paul is, he's never forgotten his roots, and he never forgets his friends either. People get the wrong impression of him, but I know the truth. Paul, I wish you well.

One of my runs took me to North London. I had this 90-year-old lady in my car, and I did the run in 3.5 hours – boy, was I shifting! Luckily for me, she fell asleep in the back seat, and when she woke up, we were there at her house. She thanked me for a safe journey; if only she knew I was doing 120 down the fucking motorway! She would have had a heart attack had she woken up.

One night, I was out on the road when the desk clerk asked me if I wanted a long run, and – as it was my turn – I said yes. We don't get to find out where we're going until we accept the job, and this run was to pick up a 15-year-old girl in Swalwell, next to the Metrocentre, and take her to Stranraer to meet her mother. That was a journey and a half – she was quoted £300 and the pickup wasn't until 11.30 pm.

Well, on the way up, we got talking. It seemed she was living in Dumfries with her foster parents, and they had accused her of pinching £500 from them, so she'd ended up in Swalwell at some mate's house.

Before doing a long journey like that, I would always take the money upfront – that way, I knew I was getting paid. Anyway, quite a while up the road, she decided to call into a garage. I stayed in the car, but before she came back – as I had my night's takings on me, plus the money she'd given me for the fare – I decided to take it all out of my pocket, except for £20. I had a drawer under my seat, so that's where the money went. This was due to the fact that her phone kept ringing and the destination was changed three times – which was suspicious. This way, if they were going to rob me at the other end, they would only get £20. Also, she said that she hadn't taken the money from the foster parents, but she paid me in Scottish notes.

On the way up, her phone rang, and she said it was her foster parents asking if she had a knife on her. I asked her, "Do you have a knife on you?" and she said no. Once again, her phone went, and this time it was her mother – to change the destination yet again. Now we had to meet them just outside Stranraer on the main road.

By this time, it was 2 am, so I was starting to get a bit worried. I rang my sister and said I was on the way to Stranraer with this young woman; then I explained how her foster parents thought she had a knife on her, knowing my sister would ring the police and get them to meet me at the drop-off point. About fifteen minutes later, sure enough, Mary rang me to say that the police would meet me just outside of Stranraer.

Well, when I got there, there was no sign of the police, but the lass's mother pulled up in a car with her boyfriend. They quickly got her daughter, and off they went – and boy was I relieved. I was quite shaken really, as I didn't know what to expect.

Ten minutes went by, and hey – the police finally turned up. I said, "You're a bit late; they've gone." I eventually got home at seven in the morning.

Beryl Armstrong

I worked for Dunston Taxis for another few years, and then, in 2001, I had a head-on smash with a stolen car being chased by the police. The car came screaming around the corner, bounced off a car at the top, and then headed on into me. The driver ran off while the passenger was still in the car.

I couldn't get out of the car as I couldn't move my legs; the fire brigade wanted to cut the roof off my car, and although I didn't let them, I probably should have, as it seemed to take forever to get me out.

I was off work for the next two years, as every time I went out on the road, I stopped as soon as I heard a siren – it didn't matter whether it was fire, ambulance, or police… I just stopped, even on roundabouts.

It was a long time before I got back to work, especially as, in 2002, I lost my eldest sister to a brain tumour. I was very close with her, closer even than I was with my twin, so it was a really terrible time.

I finally went back to taxi driving, but it just wasn't the same. So, in 2008, I saw an advert to train to work with people with learning difficulties, and I worked with them until 2010, when I retired.

Chapter Eleven

In 2012, I started to bleed. After having a partial hysterectomy, I thought to myself: This isn't right. I'm 63. I shouldn't be bleeding. So, I went to the doctors and they took some swabs, and it came back that I had an infection. They gave me antibiotics, but after taking the course, it was still the same. Then they sent me to see a consultant, who examined me and took more swabs, and the results came back, once again, that it was an infection.

I was at the doctor's every week until, in June 2013, I had an MRI scan. The next day, I had to go and see a consultant – this time at a different hospital – and while I was waiting, a nurse came up to me and asked, "Have you got anyone with you?" I said yes and then went into the consultant's room, where five of them were sitting. I knew as soon as the nurse asked me if I had someone with me that it wasn't good news.

The consultant said, "I am so sorry to tell you, but you have cancer." I said, "I could have told you that in 2012."

Anyway, I had the usual operation and chemotherapy, but because I'd already had cancer for eight months, I had to have the strongest chemo they could give me. And now here I am, nine years later.

The consultant did say that I would last for about fifteen years, which takes me to 2028 – but that's not going to happen. He also said that, had I waited another week, I would have been dead, as my fallopian tube was bursting.

I have put this in my book to warn others: if you're bleeding or have an offensive smell, get it checked. I am glad I persisted with the doctors, especially as I still have a massive bucket list to get through.

I hope you enjoyed reading my book as much as I enjoyed writing it. Everything printed in this book is absolutely true.

So, here's to the next few years – and to my completed bucket list!

Beryl Armstrong

The Trials and Tribulations of a Female Taxi Driver

Beryl Armstrong

The Trials and Tribulations of a Female Taxi Driver

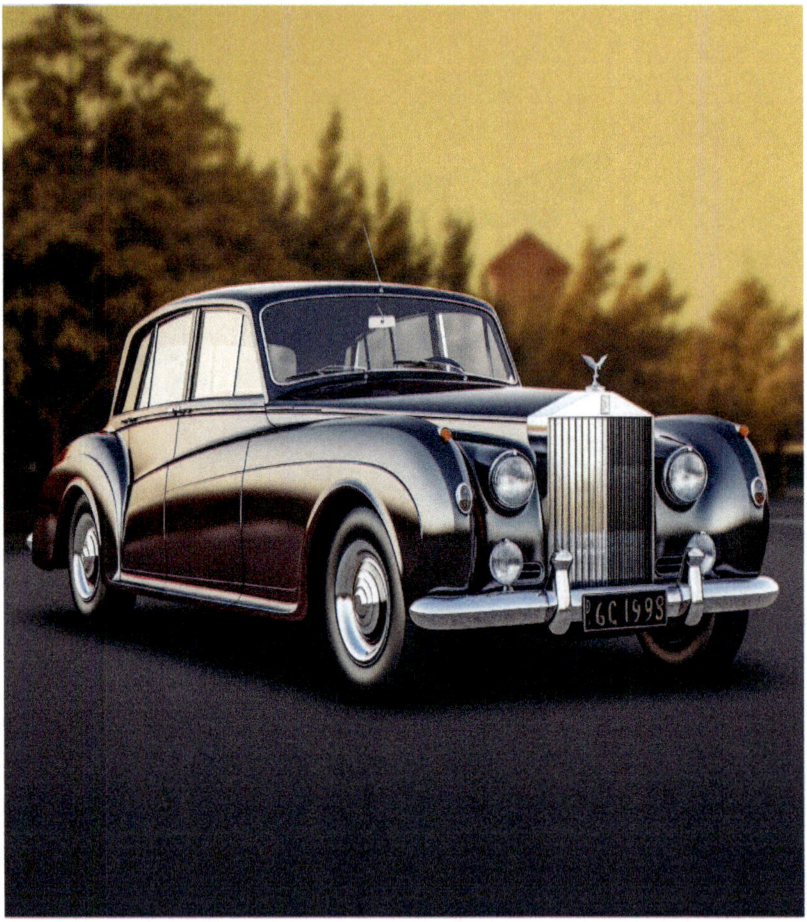